# PRAISE FOR
## *Prayer Under Eyelids*



There's this lovely way *Prayer Under*
and how it animates and brings life
ines myth and memory, the ways in w
wonder. In this work, I find a way to see grief, longing, and desire with newer eyes. Karthik is a poet who knows that someone is listening, who lets you know that he is always listening back.

**Jason Bayani**
author of *Locus*, Artistic Director of Kearny Street Workshop

The breadth of diaspora is not simply measured by miles, flights, and remittances—as Karthik Sethuraman shows in *Prayer Under Eyelids*, this gap can be represented more miniaturely as the distances that separate one from one's mother, one's father, and their own parents. Here is diaspora as a negative space that must be filled by either yearning or intimacy. Karthik is a curator of the residue tracked across migrations (in this case, that of the Tamil diaspora). By turns sensuous and fabulist, tender and traced by a subtle violence, these poems are the trail of a seeker who practices love as a manner of piety.

**Ken Chen,**
author of *Juvenilia*, Cullman Fellow at the New York Public Library

# Prayer Under Eyelids

Karthik Sethuraman

**NOMADIC PRESS**

**OAKLAND**

111 FAIRMOUNT AVENUE
OAKLAND, CA 94611

**BROOKLYN**

475 KENT AVENUE #302
BROOKLYN, NY 11249

WWW.NOMADICPRESS.ORG

**MASTHEAD**

*FOUNDING AND MANAGING EDITOR*
J. K. FOWLER

*ASSOCIATE EDITOR*
MICHAELA MULLIN

**MISSION STATEMENT**

Nomadic Press is a 501 (C)(3) not-for-profit organization that supports the works of emerging and established writers and artists. Through publications (including translations) and performances, Nomadic Press aims to build community among artists and across disciplines.

**SUBMISSIONS**

Nomadic Press wholeheartedly accepts unsolicited book manuscripts. To submit your work, please visit www.nomadicpress.org/submissions

**DISTRIBUTION**

Orders by trade bookstores and wholesalers:
Small Press Distribution,
1341 Seventh Street
Berkeley, CA 94701
spd@spdbooks.org
(510) 524-1668 / (800) 869-7553

***Prayer Under Eyelids***


This book was made possible by a loving community of chosen family and friends, old and new.

For author questions or to book a reading at your bookstore, university/school, or alternative establishment, please send an email to info@nomadicpress.org.

Cover artwork and author portrait by Arthur Johnstone

Published by Nomadic Press, 111 Fairmount Avenue, Oakland, CA 94611

First printing, 2021

Printed in the United States of America

LIBRARY OF CONGRESS CATALOGING-IN-PUBLICATION DATA

Karthik Sethuraman 1993 –
Title: *Prayer Under Eyelids*
P. CM.
Summary: *Prayer Under Eyelids* begins and ends with a child. In between, the poems, prayers, and notes in the collection explore migration, loss, and coming-of-age in a landscape where home is just over the horizon but always out of reach.

[1. POETRY. 2. CHILDHOOD. 3. MIGRATION. 4. AMERICAN GENERAL.] I. III. TITLE.

LIBRARY OF CONGRESS CONTROL NUMBER: 2021932314

ISBN: 978-1-7363963-7-7

# Prayer Under Eyelids

Karthik Sethuraman

NOMADIC PRESS

# CONTENTS

# INTRODUCTION

I began writing the poems in *Prayer Under Eyelids* after an afternoon trip to Aardvark Books on Church Street just off the J line. The first poem I wrote was titled *Notes for My Love*. In it, a speaker recounts his parent's arranged marriage and how they made sense of their suddenly shared universe. *Notes for My Love* was pseudo-autobiographical. Like in the poem, my parents had an arranged marriage and lived in changing environments across multiple continents. Most importantly, they also built a rich understanding of the world around them. But when I shared that poem with my parents, they noted a blanketing strangeness, a lot of things out of place and time. A song from a movie appeared in the wrong decade. An idiom was in the wrong language. A scene took place in an apartment where none of us had lived. *Notes for My Love* didn't make it past early drafts, but it did reveal the path I had set out on. I wanted to explore my own internal and possibly fictional conceptions of childhood, family, and home.

Along the way, I kept encountering the strangeness my parents pointed out: the tensions between sameness and estrangement, of how a person is both formed by and pushed away from their origins. Some of these tensions came from immigration, from being raised in a language and culture distinct from my parents'. Others were related to time and distance. As I kept writing *Prayer Under Eyelids*, the strangeness grew into different speakers and voices. My relationship to most of these speakers was just coincidental. This created a tension too: a tension between fiction and memory.

I spent most of my time mapping out these tensions, drawing against landscapes populated with children and their parents and grandparents. I wanted to map out how I and the speakers in my poems had navigated these tensions, where they looked in times of loss, how they spoke across enormous gaps, and what they prayed for and why. I was lucky to come

across eyelids for the title poem, *Prayer Under Eyelids*. Across drafts and revisions, eyelids seemed to embody how I could separate the internal and unseen from the external and seen. From there, the collection grew to contain poems about cremation and waking, a car breaking down in California, an apartment complex with dandelions, and more.

In cataloguing all these pieces, historical and imagined, and sharing them with you, I hope to construct an alternate world, a world where a child can split time across places, rebuild language and home, and negotiate belonging within different families and communities.

# SCAVENGER, CARRY ME HOME

what has saved me
more than the bolted
door   the flickering
lamp   the picture of
the going in a wallet
the picture of the gone
on a wall   the last pair
of socks beneath a pillow
the leaves carried in by kin
the map with treasure
mislabeled dirt

I search for keys
whisper into the lock
*do you know*
*where home is*

                                        *the tin*
*bucket lowered into a well*

*and beyond?*

                    *alone on a ledge*
*a child pulling*
                    *pulling pulling*

Some nights,
dreaming, I step again into the small boat

that carried us out and watch the bank receding—
my back to where I know we are headed.

Natasha Trethewey

*

The place to which old age carries us is neither a loneliness nor a sadness but an inlet where a motorized boat in full dress floats quietly on the water.

Yasushi Inoue

# BENEDICTION

Anthony of Padua writes,
So that we may be able to find
the face of the Lord
which we have lost,
let us light a lamp and
search the house diligently.

*

Lord, the space between me
and the next living thing
has shrunk to the size of a fingerprint.
My grandmother smuggles mangoes
into this country and when stopped,
spells the only three words she knows
—sorry, please, God.
We fit neatly into a ninety-nine Corolla,
run the engine in the parking lot,
with each sputter mouth *jeya jeya.*
A teacher walks up to the window,
open the classroom door, asks us
what we're expecting. A sunrise.
My mother's hysterectomy.
The morning after, I shatter my arm
carrying our leftover parts, and
my father holds my ulna in place,
drives me to the emergency room,
finds a vending machine, but I mistake
doctor for priest and keep counting
down to Sunday school.
We try the airport chapel next.

I'm holding onto you, Lord,
by your smallest finger.
When asked for port of entry,
my answer changes. Sometimes, it's the
K-Mart by the Rahway train station.
Once, I wrote down the exact location
of the wall where I spray painted
my name. These are special
preparations for inspection:
layers of lead, noontime prayers,
progressions around the moon.
A boy with a missing piece
is received in the mail, re-packaged
in cardboard, shipped back to his factory.
Does he hear the knock at the door?
Someone's written my name on the wall,
and every conversation is just precautionary.
A man only wants to let us know
that it can be difficult adjusting.
Things were going so well.
He's seen us at the temple
sitting by the stairs, drawing
shapes in the air. How is the son of
a beachhead and a crossing, a mosquito
or worse, when did he discover
the two kinds of people,
the ordained and the arrived. Lord,
the only time we rested by the stairs,
my mother crouched next to me
and asked if I'd like to go back home,
and if I pointed to you, Lord,
I must have whispered
which one.

# PRAYER MISTAKING SILENCE FOR LOVE

Which words when given to me
will taste metallic in my mouth

before buying groceries
must I pray

must I pray for milk

for its shape mixing in the mouths
of different men

for the word itself
on the lips of the brave

for my way of coming to terms
with my sister and
the feathers tucked into her hair

the song marching through
my mother's tongue

the beaks kissing her hands and
the hands of her love my father
watching his father

in a frame tying eggshells
around his mother's neck

it goes down easy
blood chilled just right
and who am I to ask about truancy

the only day I skipped school
I found a goose in our backyard

huddled over hatchlings suckling them
or maybe my biology is wrong

but I remember
asking my mother to leave out milk
and her lukewarm reply

*honey, don't you know to save yourself*
*for those who can use you.*

## FINGERPRINT AS GUIDE WIRE

Ink leaks into fingers when words
          won't do leaks into nails
unchewed if any remain but

          my mother, she swears she tried to
salvage me, my worthwhile parts     fed me
calcium                    supplements ground
sweat to coat my hands

                    before I slept     & each
child, cast from parents' palms, rough hands
          grooves etched from splatter
so we cover ourselves in what ails us to salve

the burns          by Saturday
                    the scent of acetone lingers,
floats through the house looking for edges
to sanitize

          portraits to manicure     my mother,
she coats herself with duties spills herself
into me          deposits fragmentsclaws

in gums, a distraction               when I
wake, I count my fingers
          find ones yet untouched     & I

am the taste of sweat on the tongue,
the taste of sweat on another's because

I take after my mother, can dress myself

in sheer
abstractions          their residues

of touch  & the crisp blueness
of rollerball kissing skin
hands carrying in her

yesterdaysound of mortar,
pestle          faint rigor

& each extremity hanging
surviving
demanding

# NOTES ON WAKING

Hushed to embers,
to a final syllable of ash,
a flame. Can I call it a reminder? A prayer?
Some time has passed since my father and sister
drove to the hospital, and I haven't silenced anything,
haven't hidden from any emergency. I swear
I've asked for safe passage
even when I don't believe in highwaymen.
My father does and with every hour
he lowers himself, and every absence
is polluted with some kind of news.
When the surgeon spoke to us, I blessed
every mention of my mother's name but
sometimes double blessed
and stuttered. At Woodbine Elementary,
my speech therapist explained that
some children find things they can't articulate
and hold themselves, stretch each sound
into a question, a prayer.
When my mother opens her eyes,
her first look is to my father
who smiles like we do when we can't hurt
the ones we love, so she looks to me.
Years ago, when we watched the weather,
my mother would complain about partial
promises of sunshine and passing clouds.
We could still be that simple,
my mother after a few days in bed
rising and reanimating, another forecast
beginning where this one ends.
I haven't held my words

for a long time now, and I don't intend to,
but she shakes her head, saves herself
for another day. I don't know if
she still tampers with smoke detectors
or lines them under her mattress.
If she'd let me, I might have lifted
her shoulder, traced the route
of the arsonists and what they burned,
their great fires.
One day, she'll tell me
I never could lie to her
but how could I—
she's sleeping on her side,
and I rustle her from the dream,
a fire engine in the late afternoon,
a girl on top running, rushing, and she asks
why I woke her now.
I say someone had to.

## KURUVI

Older now, the sparrow God gave my grandmother
in place of succulence. An ordinary thing to hold
her wants, flesh and spine and texture beneath
the bleaching sky. She asked to not be left alone
and unremarkable, to be more than the sparse words
scattered in her song. But her bird can sing, can't it?
Keep in water, seal itself tight? I shouldn't but
I hold this from her, that I know she only begged
for sustenance and in turn received a shovel,
a bag of seeds, a cage, her sparrow swallowed
by the din of buses, arguments on her doorstep,
the phone company laying a line past her toes,
and she says what is it about need that we each
must listen for some echo, never really knowing
if we are the prayer or the promise.

# FIRST RAIN

Buckets, aluminum tumblers,
containers you collect
to welcome the season

& place under the holes
you made with the pressure cooker,
the hand-me-down recipe,

the monsoon feast,
that time you fried lotus roots,
one escaped, tore an opening

into the neighbor's bathroom—
you couldn't tell cooked from burnt,
but the sudden gentleness

of these drops, these words against
your lips, you sip at what you keep,
the cactus flowering

in the mid-September light,
your eyes opening slowly,
adjusting to the haze &

then you're rubbing your nose,
the sand deposited in the cracks,
sprawled on the floor

counting the holes peeking through,
& the water whistling
to a boil, the steam resting

at the cusp of the pond not yet
stepping onto shore & careful,
you trace the outline

of a cage passed down
& within, an organ,
a figure readying,

unclasping fingers &
in the distance,
the sound of timpani

# PRAYER FOR SLEEPLESS MORNINGS

One ray stretches into memory another
into fiction I occupy the space at the crossing
half-remembering half-reciting a hymn

each morning a monk asks his echo about
the night before and receives a promise he
cannot resolve he cannot retrieve what rests

in the beads on his neck the dots on his tongue
I reach my mother instead and she tells me
the moon comes before and after the sun

this is her way of telling time her hair is streaked
with vermillion she isn't permitted to perfume
herself—she gives me a list with groceries

I can determine the difference between the present
and the past by studying which items I've bought
already but now the wires cross again

a child is crying I smell smoke tears are easy
to forget over a cigarette but she doesn't smoke
a child is crying he holds a flame in his palm

I scratch camphor off the list—my mother
finishes the echo alone is a state of mind not
a state of being but before she disconnects

I stop her love is the word we use to describe
the thing that begins and ends all things.

# I SEE MY FATHER LOOK BOTH WAYS BEFORE CROSSING THE STREET

near every morning
an ashtray
just emptied
and the piercing sunlight
through the vapors

stopping to smell
the jasmine bent
over the fence
what impossible
effort to arrive

our lips green inside
like we've forgotten
ourselves in the
glove compartment

like the crossing guard
with the cigarette in her mouth

like her shadow
between ours
larger and smaller

we separate and our arms
catch and we pull
at our wholeness

what abundance
of caution

if the sky faintly
flashes we freeze

if the crossing guard
extinguishes
her smoke we disintegrate

our remembrances
tidy and well-proportioned

will we remain unglued if
someone calls from across
the street

if the crossing guard
finds us tomorrow
not hand in hand

if the cigarette falls
from her lips

if she whispers *take care*
or *be safe*

the words we want
but cannot speak
to ourselves

# CARAPACE

From the sunwashed photograph my father kept, smoke
and what all I knew of death, how little a person
leaves behind and how my father's mother might embrace her son
despite everything he would never know like the size
his father would become after everyone returned home
and how small a memory would be when stored in porcelain
and how one day his father would've been just like him,
with a child and a newspaper open on his lap,
pointing to the attractions in some place they would never go,
and how his mother would call them for evening prayer
and how his father would lift him to ring
the brass bell before the altar,
the altar burning away.

# PRAYER UNDER EYELIDS

Little crow,   you keep warm in
  your mother's hair   her swallows
humming in your cheek   you're
  not a doctor   not a priest
but keep slowness   keep virtue
  and length and weight and the elms
that no longer babble   your reflection
  in indigo carrying irises   the brook
that separates you   that stamps this
  place with a familiar name, within
the reach of some crumbling god
  before you could move you imagined
each terror as your mother   and now
  keeping shelf stable prayer books
a casket   a labeled one   each thing
  lowering you   cleaving you   even
your shadow peeking in through the
  top of the window   boarded up.

# THE RIVER



When I dig a hole and can't bury myself,
I leave an opening to collect stray moonbeams, carry a portable
television to monitor the eight o'clock news. Reach me through
the cable station, I'm watching for the vernal rains

much like my grandmother before she was cast into the river,
waiting in pieces, teeth in a cup, kidneys tumbling locks, kidneys
turning grey. Through her keyholes, light left a residue, peeling,
a flailing hope and its jackfruit flesh, the carcass washed up on the bank,

the scent of my grandmother's hands the last time in the ambulance, my father holding
her smallest finger up the stairway, the alley between the pharmacy and the internet cafe.
I pretend he told his siblings, over the telephone, that to love is to love alone.
When she went, sheathed in her own blanket, catching a glimpse

of my grandfather walking down the hall, the dial on the fan pushed to rotate,
to keep the eyes away, and her youngest son, my father in the next room,
the kitchen, blending rice and yogurt with salt, did she look down, did she
see her footprints in the dirt next to theirs, her marks on the floors of her home.

## CUB AND WOLF

My mother marks me
a traitor  it's in my blood
my great grandfather harbored
imperialists  how can I hope
to bleed  what does she mean
when she says we do what we need
to survive  I hear a child crying
next door  his mother shushes
rattles his pacifier  will he object
can he  will he do what he needs
to survive  can he remember
this conversation overheard
through a wall  does blood
remember cloth and bone

will she believe him if he tells her
their pain is the same across water
he whispers instead  whispers
I will not make out but imagine
inwardly a knife sharpened
hands bare  shavings falling slowly
then at once  and I'm peeling myself
trying to cut through hide  my shell
moving from hallway to hallway
leaning against whatever gathers
with each sliver my lips asking
instead asking what she means
when she says we do what we are
we live when we bleed

# MY MOTHER, INTO SAND

*I hope he will take me to a place*
*with fewer galleries fewer doors.*

**Jorge Luis Borges**

my mother
carries us
in her
shoulders

we can't see
her ache

how she walks
meticulously

are we what
she wants

we are
offerings
to God

is a statement
at intervals
grain by grain,

spilling from
her back,

reconstituting
her body

I can't see
they are too
small—pieces
I can't pick up

and offerings
to God

of fact
collecting

collecting
each moment
piecing together
her likeness,

before her
—waiting here
past the dunes

we move
in decades

materializing
collapsing

# COUNTRY ROADS

I frame family portraits.
Colors fade but faces remain.

Most are returned in time, but some missing
I carry in search of resemblance,

and one I've kept with me awhile,
its weight in cracks aging

to black and blue.
Weary and careful, a column

of sentries, I balloon my stomach.
Measure circumference with a compass.

Inside, a little death.
A mother's apple pie refrigerated, reheated.

Left out before labor day weekend.
On moonless nights,

a boy offers coffee, grain liquor, sighs.
I go to meet his teacher,

a funeral parlor conversation
sun overhead, *truant*.

Twice in two nights
I cough up the pulp of

his mother's letters. I can't

keep down what I read.

He brings me her cooking,
steamed rice and beets,

black mustard seeds.
Two stitches mark treasures,

one retrieved, another buried
between my hips.

I save myself for the close,
here's the sign.

Between navel and hip,
fingers dug deep in flesh,

sometimes I hurt
more when let go.

*

I treasure my father's stomach
like my own. I see him over

the gully. His feet in tan slippers.
His feet in water. His hair bristles

against the algae. He holds himself
by his vertebrae. Palms flush against

the gaps in his intestines. Back
sweat-poor. He doesn't know how

many photographs he has left. If
he does, he doesn't dare count.

A few years ago, he gave me an
almanac. The fourth page read

the progression of stomach
circumference in south asian men.

We squint more now than we used to,
carry each other in our eyelids, glimpse

a distorted moon. Small near the prairies.
Huge near the stars, and age is a series

of shoes we step into. Now, he is fifteen,
breaks his wrist on concrete. I am six and

cry when he promises me tomorrow.
At twenty two, I hold my breath,

shoulders arching outward, but by
our third date, I reveal I am the son

of a cavity, opening myself to demonstrate,
stuffing as much into my stomach

as I can, but I still reach the theater
before the operation begins.

I think this is love. Something
cavernous. Scars on either side of

our navels, we balloon into the gap
between us. Hands at ease on our hips.

## PRAYER WITH GOLDEN BUFFALO

*As for the buffalo,*
*it stuck like a leech*
*to the stork's feet–*
*all for love.*

**Solaikkili**

Mirror ~~and wipe~~ my tears
covered in humid nights
~~a touch!~~ a lump in my throat
my ~~beginning~~ becoming a social endeavor
do I remember ~~fondly?~~ that time I hid
in the bathroom holding up the line for
old men ~~and their shits~~
my fingers wet from clenching
sweat called easy desperation
my nephew ~~warns me~~ asks me
~~who am I leaving for, where am I running to~~
isn't home the place where the food
smells ~~at least~~ the most like my memories
a ~~golden~~ buffalo to
bathe in the river with lotuses
one day a man breaks ~~himself into~~ me
fills me with ~~breaths of~~ stolen things
and ~~to be~~ shocked into hope
is that called alarm ~~alarm!~~
and I confuse all lamplight ~~for purpose~~
and where is my white stork
~~to love~~ to leap into
when I replace ~~a part of~~ myself
with the immaterial it hardens
scabs over what I've lost
my love ~~kept from~~
the ether which makes me

# PIECEMEAL

A car stops moving, we sell it for parts. Doesn't matter
the chipped driver side handle, the duct tape passing
smog tests. I drove it for another thousand miles after
the check engine light burned out, drove it up to Philo
and stopped at the garage. Not up to your standards,
or mom's, but someone has to go on. Didn't expect this
poem to become parenthetical, was just checking in, but
we shift from frame to frame and at night drop the mirror,
rearview a tight curve, a mountain, a deed linking my name,
yours. Mechanic said not worth fixing so I found another one.
Don't make them like this anymore. Stalled off ninety-nine
near Mariposa and I pushed it until the radio came back on,
played Madonna like an anthem. I'm naming all these places
so you know where we've been, where you've wanted to go,
and holding on is easy. I count signposts, learn landmarks,
and if the air conditioner comes on, I allow a little catharsis,
bleed it out until it's ready. Shouldn't have fought so hard,
wasn't good in the thunder, trembling, but maybe one last
night, and I can't think of a better way to go, next to you
like a shape in the sky, mist then cloud then star through
the dappled windshield.

## SARAMAKAVI

*TRADITIONAL TAMIL ELEGIES AND LAST RITES, THEY WERE ORIGINALLY WRITTEN ON PALM LEAVES AND CIRCULATED WITHIN VILLAGES AFTER FUNERALS. THEY RECORD BOTH THE INTIMATE AND MUNDANE DETAILS OF THE LIVES OF ORDINARY PEOPLE.*

### 1. TELESCOPE

Marker or no
marker, I wanted the orbit
of the world to account for me.

Impediment,
displacement, clink-
clank a thud, stopping at the edge

of a body.
A corpse. Should've said
a carcass. The carcass of so and so,

would've one
day been a such and such.
How awful, the parents on the street

wailing. There's
a natural order to things.
Boy breaks in. Body begets a body.

Is begotten by
or from. A body which
maps each yes and no to some

question it answers.
What space is measured?
Yes. And operating the engine?

No. How much
left in the tank? No. The
chance a body outlasts a body. No.

I grew tired of
asking so I took my bones
and lodged them in the mechanism

of the earth,
reinforced them every chance
I had, trying to dam the slipping

light but still
the brittle dusk and me
mistaken, having spent my last spark.

How wrong I
must have been to want
the world. To want the world before

it trampled me
to acknowledge my body,
the length of time it held its form.

## 2. APARTMENT

I write from Middlesex County a brown boy
pretending to be the Undertaker and when
I suplex the Rock my playstation flickers

or is that my aunt calling on the landline
to ask where my parents are and have I lost
my language yet or am I mourning another

tragedy maybe the passing of my stillness
having hung on the clothesline an extra
week and now so dehydrated my mother

confides that she dreams of returning to
her mother and their roadside stall where
they sold shoestrings and silkworm shells

she points to a dark one and then to me
as if I am the one with soil under my nails
but when it breaks it scatters onto the stove

blackening and separating into my sugar
my seeds the thin membrane enclosing
my lips and a voice I keep searching for

and if my mother appears again and if she
calls out that I lack that I am coarse with
solid tongue and wrong like a crow that what

I can not know I grieve and the old woman
outside the gate uses a word for grandson
and I start grasping for anything that will do

a photo of my first fall or an address to the
vacant lot or a sign of where and when to turn

## 3. NIGHT

Here is my home.

A rice cooker.

A daily stain.

My mother's mother in her bed.

Rice, medium-grain, three tumbles in cold water, wipe when done.

A washing machine.

My mother's mother in her bed.

A grocery bill, a utility bill.

A closet full of bedsheets.

My mother's mother in her bed.

Neighbors who knock, their noses, their remedial pies.

A warning from the homeowner's association.

My mother's mother in her bed.

A vessel, a leak, a midnight phone call.

My mother's mother in her bed.

Here is my home.

My mother's mother in her bed.

## 4. DANDELION

My dear gullible hunger—
say someone promises me
something, anything,
the first petal stripped from
a daffodil, a peek at
tomorrow's sunset. See

how my tongue itches, how
it scoops the final ear of rice
from the sink and licks each
sentence onto burnished tin,
handprints on a tablet, taste
of lobe and ring and titanium

stud, these marks tell stories.
A boy pierced is safe in his
mother's arms but honeyed,
clothed in mosquito nets,
I have this fear of losing
myself to wholeness,

and creviced, my stems
appear, dandelions. My hair
has been stiff for some time
now. My lips, still and
transplanted, grasp at the
margins, purse away

the yellow rays, weeds—
through the blinds, clusters of
mouths, some half full, others
missing teeth and this, this
must be it—how could I go
on blaming a thing for living.

# (NOTES)

The first epigraph quotes the ending of Natasha's Trethewey's poem *Elegy* from her collection *Thrall*. The second quotes a passage from Yasushi Inoue's short story *Reeds* (translated by Michael Emmerich).

In Benediction, the passage from Anthony of Padua is excerpted from his *Sermon for the Sixth Sunday after Easter*. His words reference Luke's parable of the lost coin.

Kuruvi means sparrow in Tamil.

*My mother, into sand* opens with a passage from Jorge Luis Borges' short story *The House of Asterion* (translated by James Irby).

*Prayer with golden buffalo* is prefaced by a stanza from Solaikkili's *The Story of a Golden River* (translated by Lakshmi Holmström).

*Saramakavi* takes from a historical Tamil elegiac poetic practice, the saramakavi. In contemporary Tamil poetry, Ahilan's *Saramakavikal* utilizes this practice to confront the trauma resulting from the Sri Lankan civil war. *Saramakavi* owes much to Ahilan's work and Geetha Sukumaran's subsequent translations and studies in *Then There Were No Witnesses*.

# CLASSROOM GUIDE

## SMALL REMEMBRANCES

In poetry, the act of remembering is often tied to very specific moments. For example, a poem might remember the first time a parent takes a child to the zoo. These moments can take on larger than life significance, especially when placed within a narrative and when looking back from a distance. How do we, as custodians of memory, keep track of these small moments? Which small moments jump out to us, and what do they highlight about our own personal idiosyncrasies?

### PROMPT

Start from a small and specific memory. Describe that memory in as much detail as possible. Then, pour through the descriptions of time, place, and other people inhabiting the memory. Create a poem which teases apart these details and considers the importance of the memory. Address the pieces you may have left out of the remembrance and also the things you still carry with you.

### REPRESENTATIVE POEMS

*"I see my father look both ways before crossing the street," "Fingerprint as guide wire"*

## LETTERS TO THE SELF

In many ways, we write to communicate with our other selves. Sometimes, this takes the form of addressing an earlier or later version of the self. Sometimes, we speak through alternates, imagining ourselves as animals or landscapes. What would we say to ourselves if we had the language to reveal what we truly felt? What would we call ourselves? What do our names for ourselves mean, and how do they relate to our self-identities? Poems as letters can be powerful devices, perhaps even more so when they are written to ourselves.

### PROMPT

Begin by addressing yourself. This could be with another name, like "little crow", or with your own name. Continue the poem in the first person. Address concerns you may have with yourself, things that you've noticed are changing or different. Rewrite the poem in second person, referring to "you". Rewrite the poem in third person, referring back to the "little crow" or "the child" or another version of yourself you're addressing. Experiment with these forms of address and navigate back to the beginning, the initial address.

### REPRESENTATIVE POEMS

*"Prayer under eyelids." "Saramakavi (Dandelion)," "Scavenger, carry me home"*

## INTERGENERATIONAL DIALOGUES

Our connections span across time just as they do across space, and we so often find ourselves in conversation with both those who came before and after us. What can we learn from the people, ideas, and histories that preceded us? And what about those which are yet to be written? How can a poem work across multiple moments in time, and how might it thread together the past, the present, and the future?

### PROMPT

Pick characters which span multiple generations. This might be family members: ancestors and descendants, parents and children. This might be those you are in community with: elders and teachers, students and mentees. Speak with these characters in the same poem. Write about how they have shaped your life and how you have shaped theirs. Revisit where you may have conflicted with these individuals and how they might conflict with each other. Think about how you might all grow together across generations.

## REPRESENTATIVE POEMS

*"Cub and wolf," "Carapace," "The river"*

# ACKNOWLEDGEMENTS

Thank you to Jason Bayani, Mihee Kim, Diana Li, and the broader Kearny Street Workshop and APAture families where I found sustenance as a poet and community member; to Nora Boxer and CCSF for all the guidance as I started and continued the journey to what would become this collection; to Kevin Lu and Helena Li for all the close readings of these works in their earliest drafts.

My deepest gratitude to J. K. Fowler and Nomadic Press for believing in this collection; to Tongo Eisen-Martin for working tirelessly with me to edit and grow these works; to Preeti Vangani, Jason Bayani, Ken Chen, and Paige Lewis who saw the best in this collection and gave it their words and praise.

To my mother, my father, and my sister, who inhabit these pages as much as I do: these are our stories, hearts, and homes; I write this with the words and tongues I learned from you; I write this with all my love.

To Wei, who first listened to these poems in the back of a dimly lit bookstore, I hope to always share these pieces of myself with you and even more to share my heart.

To Kai, I began writing this before I could even imagine your being, yet it's always been for you.

I'm grateful to the editors and readers of the journals and anthologies where some of these poems first appeared, often in earlier and different forms:

"Scavenger, carry me home," "My mother, into sand," *Berkeley Poetry Review*

"Prayer mistaking silence for love," "Notes on waking," *Mud Season Review*
"Kuruvi," AAWW's *The Margins*
"First rain," *Hematopoiesis Press*
"Prayer for sleepless mornings," *Hot Metal Bridge*
"I see my father look both ways before crossing the street," *Barren Magazine*
"Prayer under eyelids," *The Rumpus*
"The river," *Fugue*
The first section of "Country roads," *Kestrel*
"Piecemeal," *Dovecote*
"Benediction," *No Tender Fences: An Anthology of Immigrant & First-Generation American Poetry*
"I see my father...," "Cub and wolf," *Enizagam's 2019 Anthology*

Sections of "Saramakavi" were written and performed at the Asian Art Museum with support from Kearny Street Workshop's Interdisciplinary Writer's Lab, and the last section ("Dandelion") first appeared in *The Comstock Review.*